Saint Nicholas

The Real Story of the Christmas Legend

Julie Stiegemeyer

Illustrated by Chris Ellison

CONCORDIA PUBLISHING HOUSE · SAINT LOUIS

For Scott and Jacob,
with love. — J.S.

A man named Nicholas lived a long time ago in a village by the turquoise sea. The village was called Myra, in a faraway country called Lycia. It was just three hundred years after Jesus walked the earth.

Every day, Nicholas swept through the village
in his long robes. A circle of children, eager for his smile,
followed him wherever he went. The children knew that
Nicholas loved them and always had a kind word for them.

For you see, Nicholas was the pastor of this village by the sea. He shared Jesus Christ's overflowing love with the people in all he said and did. He baptized them, he gave them the Lord's Supper, and he always reminded them of God's love.

One chilly day, Satka, the littlest of the village children, did not follow Nicholas when the others did. Instead, he sat crying on the stone steps of the church.

Nicholas noticed the brown-haired boy and asked gently, "Satka, where is your smile today?"

"My father is upset, Pastor Nicholas. He keeps asking, 'what will happen to my girls?'"

Nicholas dried Satka's tears and said, "Let's go talk to your father."

The tall man and the little boy walked down the dusty streets. Stone houses dotted the hillsides above the rocky cliffs by the sea. As Satka and Nicholas approached the humble home, they saw the three girls and their father.

"Patya, my dear man, I hear there is trouble," Nicholas said.

With a heavy sigh, Patya explained that his daughters wanted to get married, but they had no dowry. In those days long ago, when ladies wanted to get married, they needed money or other things of value to set up a home. This was called a dowry. But this family was very poor, and Anna, Katerina, and Lydia did not have dowries. The girls could not get married.

Nicholas looked kindly on Patya, his long-time friend. "I know you are worried. I would like to help your family. We will pray to God and trust that He will find a way."

Patya nodded. "Yes, we will pray that our Father in heaven will help my daughters."

*N*icholas prayed night after night in the candle-lit church and wondered how God's love would pour out to this family. He thought about all the good things God had given him. And he thought about God's greatest gift of all—sending Jesus to save us from our sins.

Then Nicholas had an idea.

Nicholas rose from his bed that same night
in the frosty darkness. Cloaked in fur, he struggled
against the bitter cold through the empty streets.
Soon he arrived at the house where Satka
and his sisters lived.

When he arrived at the sleeping house,
Nicholas gently pushed open the shutter that
covered the window. Very carefully he dropped
something onto the floor, taking great care to
be as quiet as possible so he didn't disturb
the family.

Then Nicholas pulled the shutter closed
and walked back home, smiling to himself
along the way.

orning came, and with it a wonderful surprise for Anna, Katerina, and Lydia. On the floor, next to their shoes, they found three bags of gold. Now they had their dowries. Now they could marry and set up homes of their own!

With tears in his eyes, Patya led his family in prayer. "Lord, from Your bounty You gave us Your own dear Son. Now Your blessings have poured out to us again. We give You thanks and praise. Amen."

In time, all three of Patya's daughters got married.
Pastor Nicholas blessed the couples and told them,
"Whenever you are sad, whenever you are afraid,
remember: God will help you."
And God always did!

Nicholas was filled with Jesus' love—
so much so that love poured out through
everything he said and did.

Tales of Pastor Nicholas's kindness
and generosity spread throughout the land.
He became known as Father Christmas.
And to this day, people continue to give gifts
at Christmas, like Nicholas did, as a way to share
God's love and show kindness to others.

*H*owever, God is even more generous and loving still! God gave us the greatest gift we could ever imagine: He gave us a Savior, Jesus Christ. At Christmas we celebrate the birth of Jesus and how He came as a baby, but eventually would die for the sins of the world. Jesus is the real gift of Christmas. And like Nicholas, we are filled with Jesus' love so we want to share that love with others.

Dear Grown-up:

Although this story is somewhat fictionalized, Nicholas is a real historical figure who lived in the fourth century. He was Bishop of Myra, a city in Lycia, Asia Minor (what is modern-day Turkey). The region is situated on the Mediterranean Sea across from Greece.

The people of Myra had already heard the Good News of the Gospel of Jesus Christ before Nicholas came to serve them. The Apostle Paul had traveled there on his mission journey. This visit is recorded in Acts 27:5–6.

As a Christian, Nicholas suffered persecution under the Roman Emperor Diocletian and was imprisoned until Constantine came into power and showed tolerance to Christians.

Tales of Nicholas's generosity were widespread, and he became patron saint of Russia. In Europe, he was known as Father Christmas, and in America, Santa Claus. Legends about his home at the North Pole, flying reindeer, and distributing gifts all over the world on Christmas Eve were created to enhance his story, but his generosity is based in historical fact. The story of his supplying the dowries for the three girls is believed to be factual.

Nicholas's feast day (the day he died) is December 6th. Many families observe St. Nicholas Day by having the children in the home place their shoes by the door when they go to bed the night before. When they awaken on the morning of December 6, their shoes are filled with bags of gold foil-wrapped chocolate coins that were secretly placed there during the night.

The significance of Nicholas for us today is that his response to God's great love for us in Jesus was to care for other people. His kindness and care for children are modeled every time we give a gift out of love.

The author

Glossary

Asia Minor—A large peninsula bordered by the Black Sea on the north, the Mediterranean on the south, and the Aegean on the west. An ancient land, it was important to travelers, merchants, and government leaders. Asia Minor is the present-day Turkey.

Christian—One who believes that Jesus Christ is God in the flesh, that His birth was a miracle, and that He took the punishment for the world's sin to earn forgiveness for us. This forgiveness comes freely as a gift of faith in Christ.

Baptism—Water applied with the name of the Triune God to a person in a saving act of God where He washes away sin, creates faith, and makes the person His child. Romans 6 tells us that in Baptism, we die with Christ and rise to new life in Him.

Dowry—An amount of money, goods, or property that a wife presented to a husband upon their marriage. A dowry was used to set up the household for the new couple.

Generosity—The quality of giving freely of one's possessions, time, or other.

Father Christmas—Another name for Santa Claus, Father Christmas is a legendary man who delivers gifts to children at Christmas.

Lord's Supper—A celebration in church of the presence of Jesus in His body and blood under bread and wine. This Holy Feast is where Christ's church gathers to receive the gifts of forgiveness of sins and salvation.

Lycia—An ancient country in the Roman Empire, Lycia was a mountainous coastal country. People have been living on this land since the 14th century B.C.

Myra—The capital of Lycia, Myra was an important seaport in the Roman Empire. The apostle Paul visited Myra during his mission journeys. It is known today for its ancient Roman ruins and beautiful setting.

Pastor—A man called by God to a local congregation to serve the people there with the gifts from God: the preached Word, Baptism, and the Lord's Supper.

Paul—An apostle, Paul was converted to Christianity after Christ's death and spent the remainder of his life preaching, teaching, and helping to build the Christian church.

Prayer—Words or thoughts we offer to God. A Christian prays because the Bible assures us that God keeps His promises, forgives us, hears us, and answers us. We can pray about anything and God promises to answer according to His will, not ours.

Saint—This is a word from the Greek language that means "holy one". A Christian is holy by faith in Christ, our Redeemer.

Turkey—A Muslim country between Greece on the west and Syria, Iraq, Iran, Armenia, and Georgia on the east. The capital city is Ankara.